This Book Belongs To:

____

BY

Home Planners And Journals

To help you organize your life

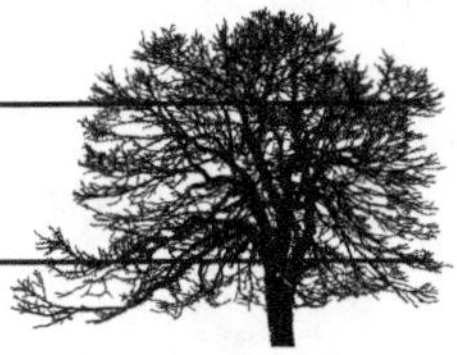

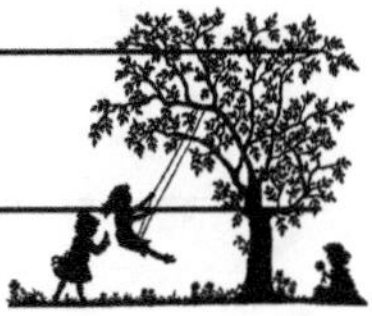

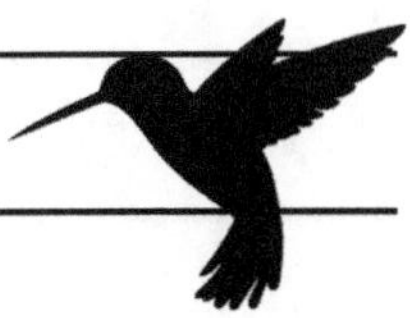

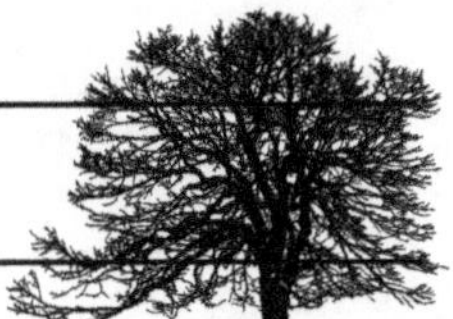

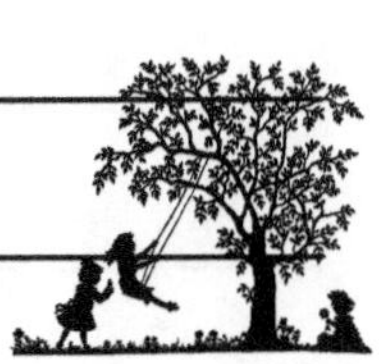

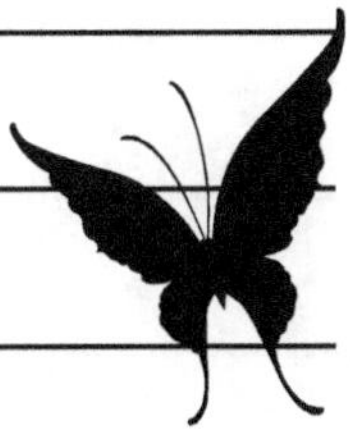

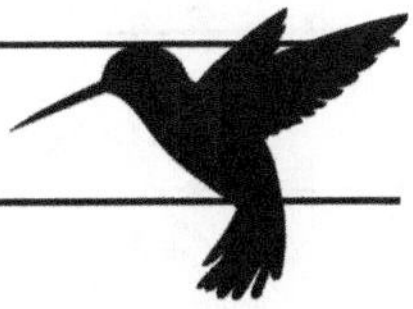

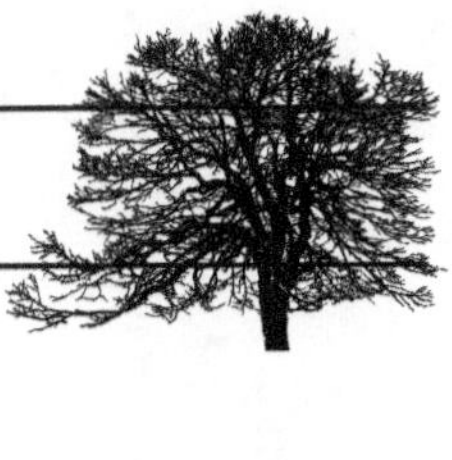

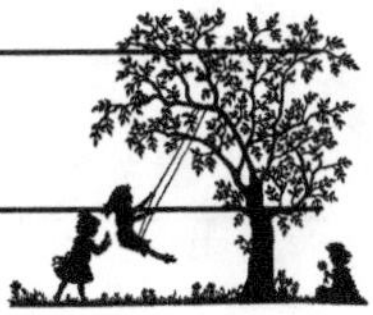

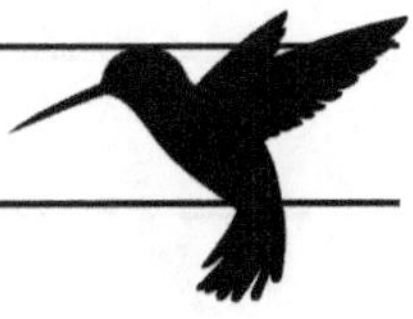

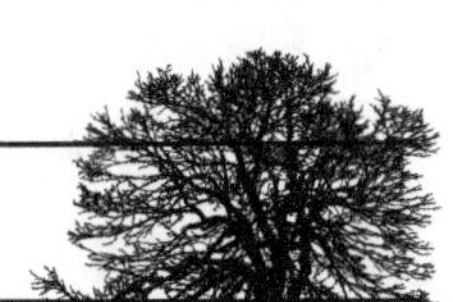

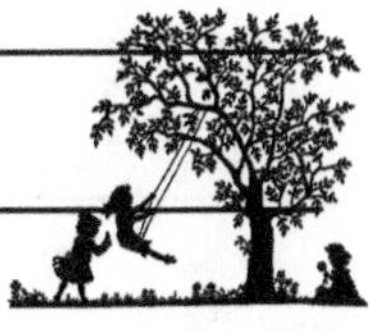

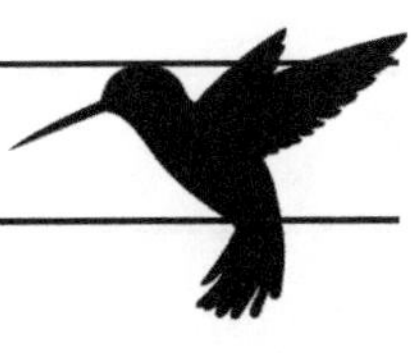

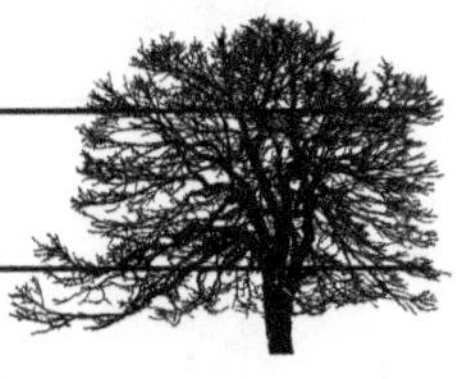

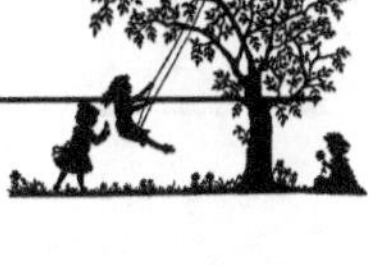

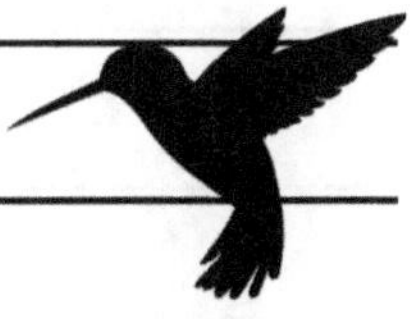

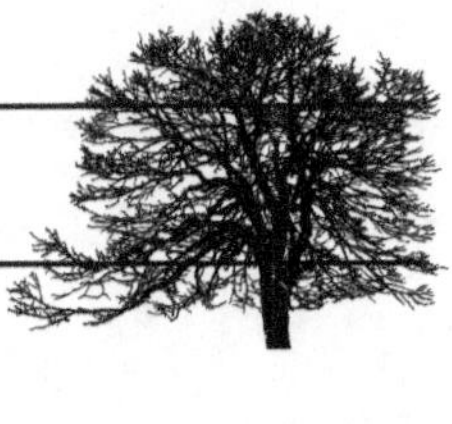

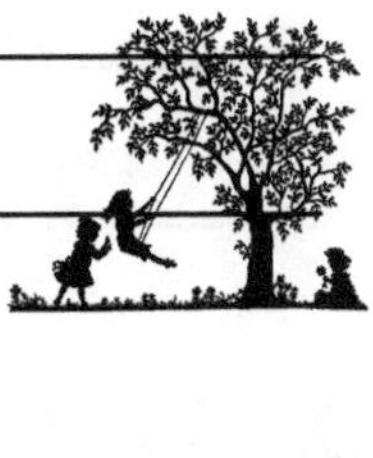

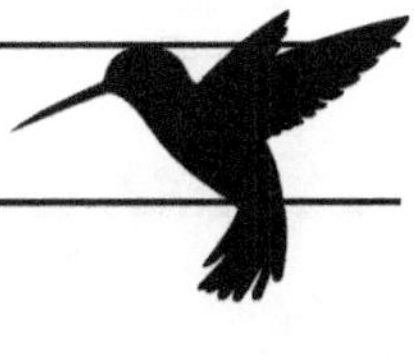

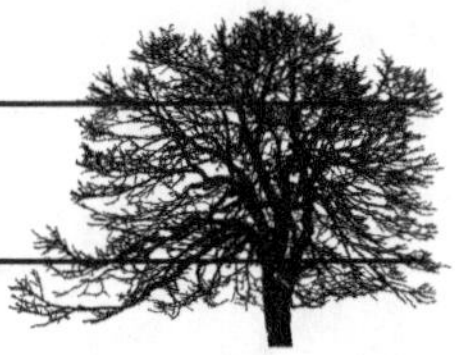

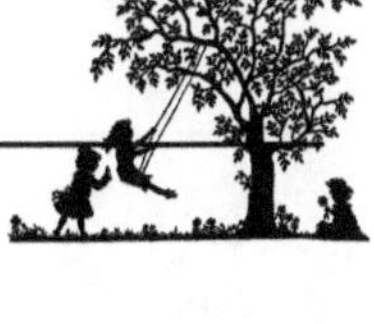

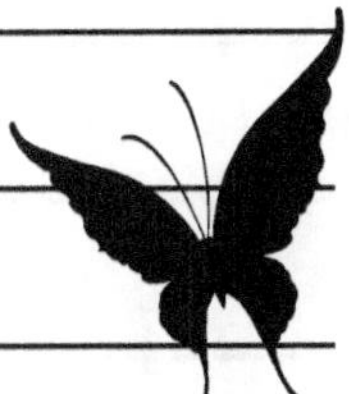

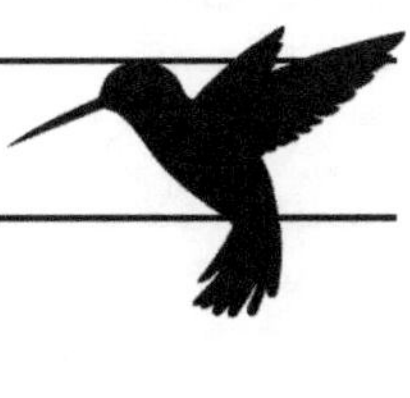

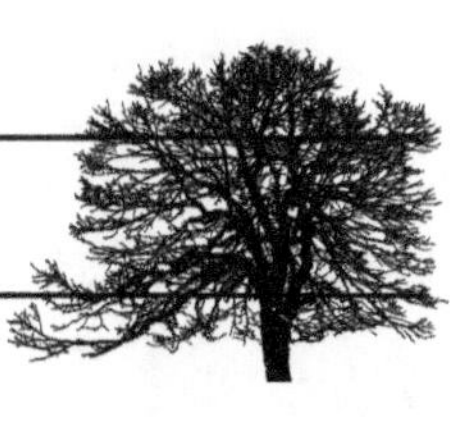

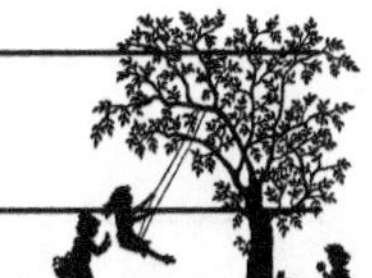

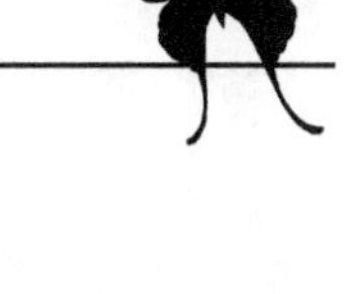

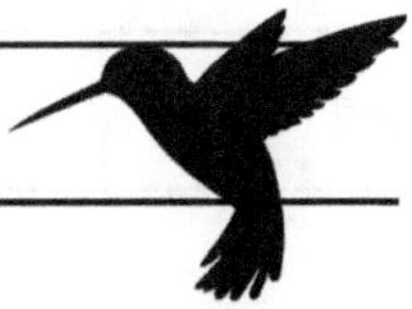

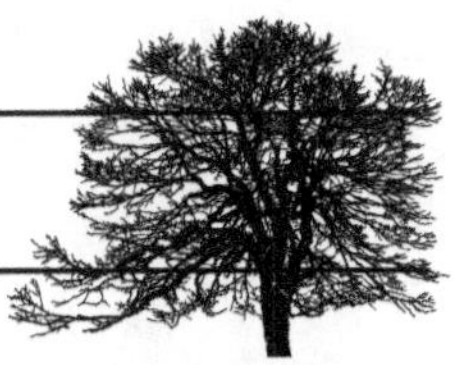

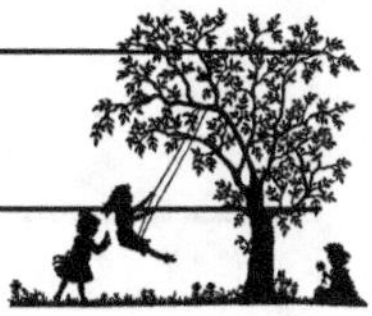

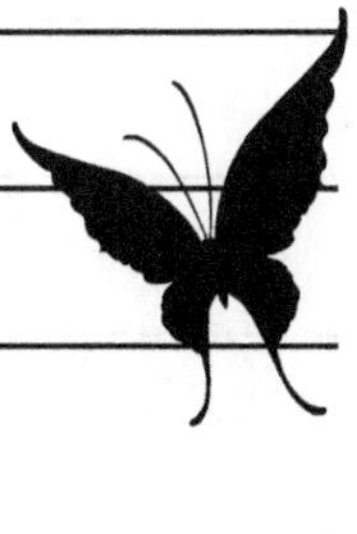

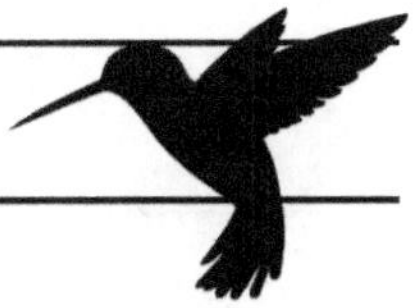

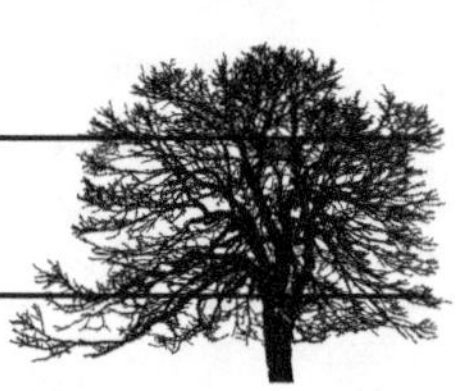

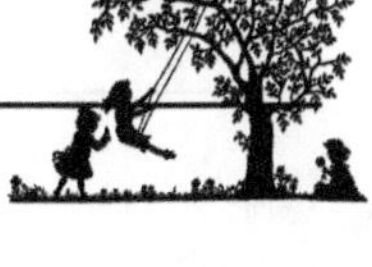

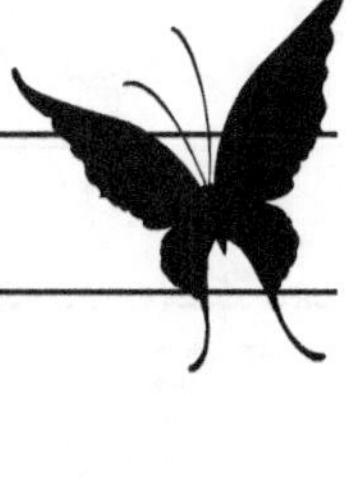

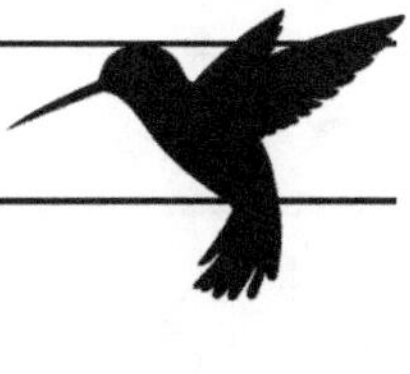

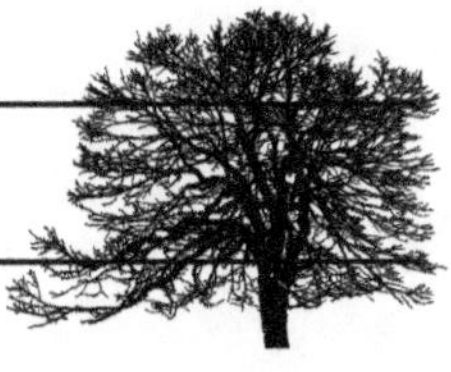

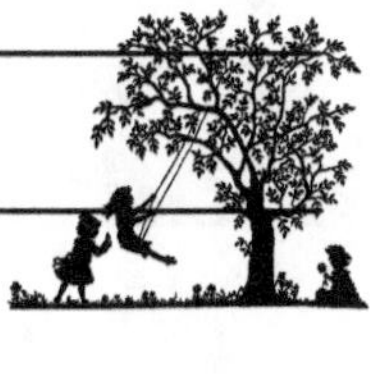

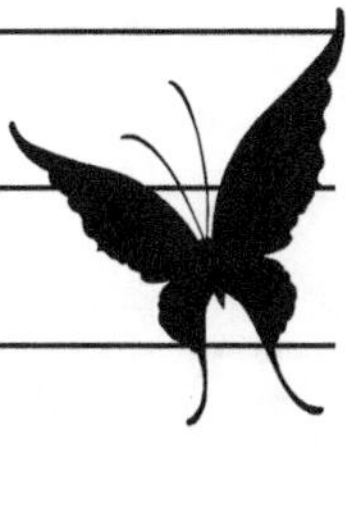

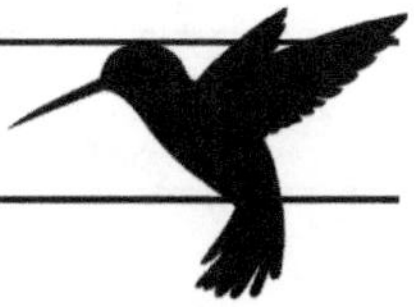

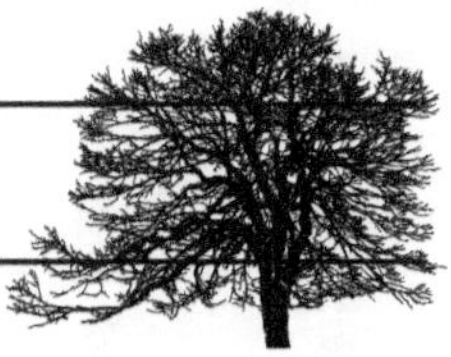

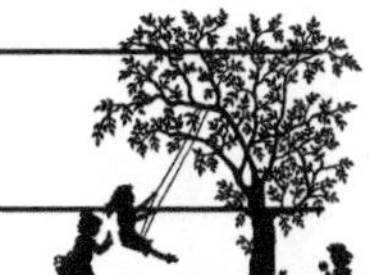

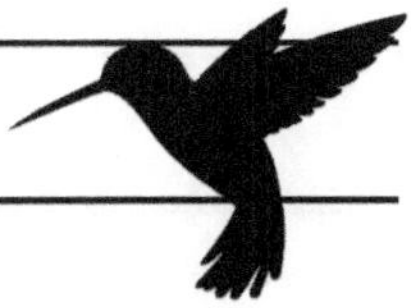

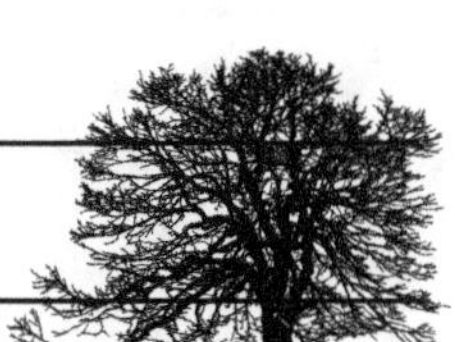

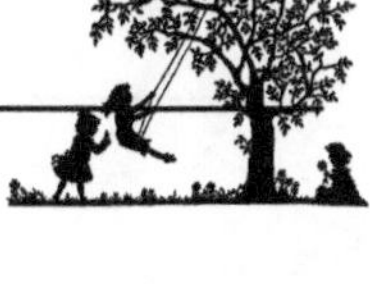

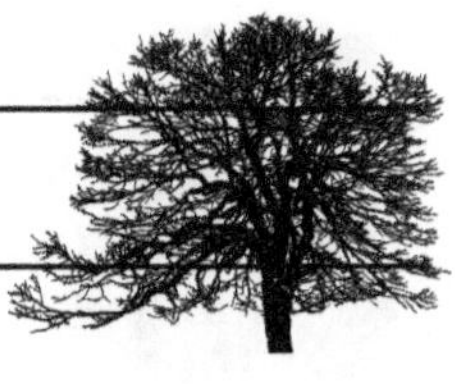

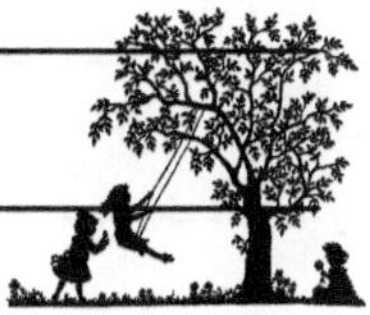

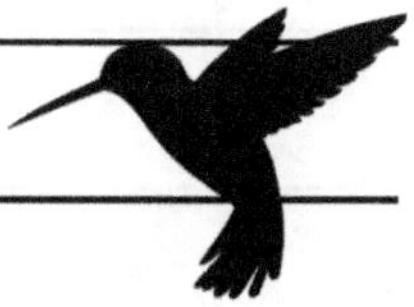

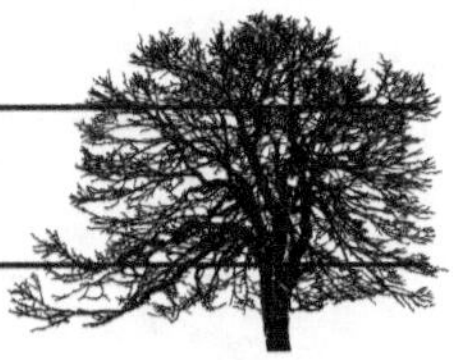

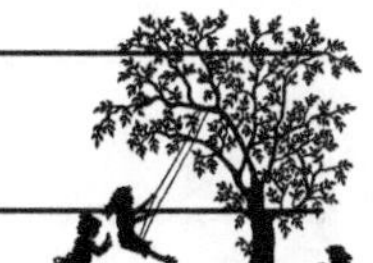

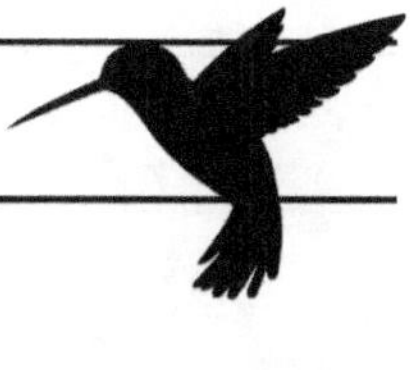

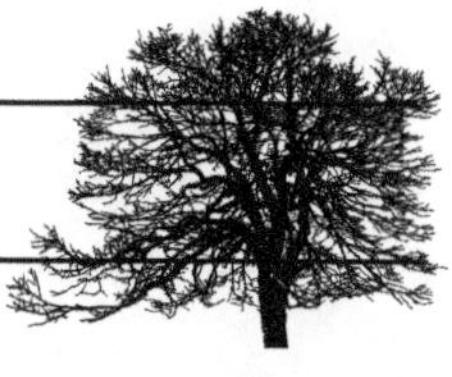

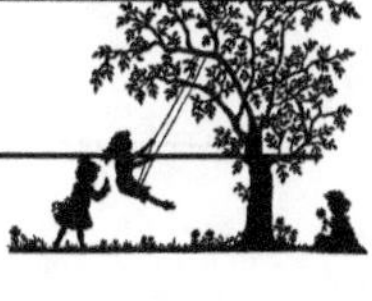

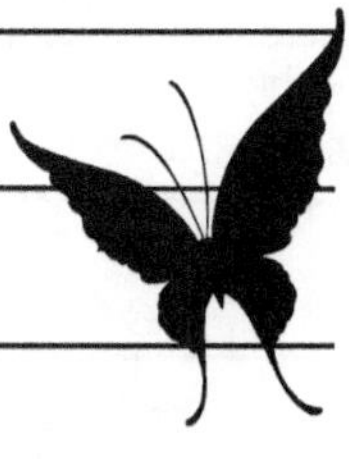

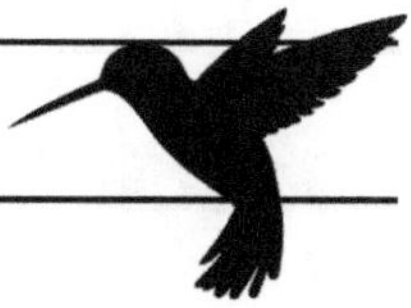

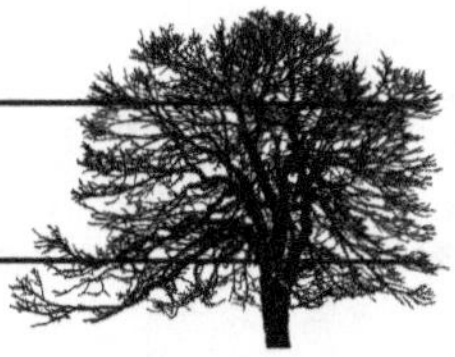

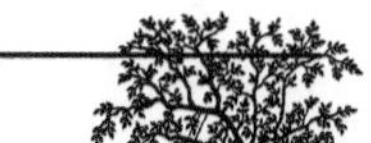

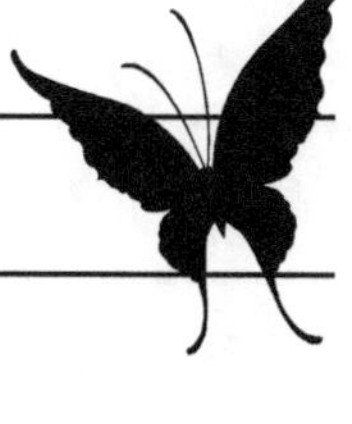

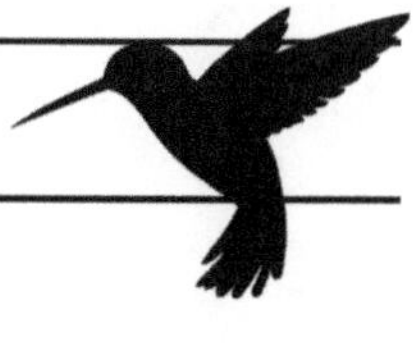

www.ingramcontent.com/pod-product-compliance
Lightning Source LLC
Chambersburg PA
CBHW050948050726
47592CB00007B/2481
* 9 7 8 1 7 9 7 5 9 9 6 4 9 *